DAT

COOL CAREERS WITHOUT COLLEGE FOR

FILM AND

TELEVISION

BUFFS

COOL CAREERS WITHOUT COLLEGE FOR
FILM AND TELEVISION BUFFS

**MELANIE
ANN APEL**

The Rosen Publishing Group, Inc.

New York

This book is dedicated to Michael Bonnell for all the love, support, and goodness I could ask for. And to Hayden Seth, for waiting as long as possible.

Published in 2002 by The Rosen Publishing Group, Inc.
29 East 21st Street, New York, NY 10010

Library of Congress Cataloging-in-Publication Data

Apel, Melanie Ann.
Cool careers without college for film and television buffs / Melanie Ann Apel.— 1st ed.
p. cm. — (Cool careers without college)
Includes bibliographical references and index.
ISBN 0-8239-3501-9 (lib. bdg.)
1. Motion pictures—Vocational guidance—Juvenile literature.
2. Television broadcasting—Vocational guidance—Juvenile literature.
[1. Motion pictures—Production and direction—Vocational guidance.
2. Television—Production and direction—Vocational guidance.
3. Vocational guidance.] I. Title. II. Series.
PN1995.9.P75 A64 2001
331.7'02—dc21

2001003050

Manufactured in the United States of America

CONTENTS

	Introduction	7
1	Actor	11
2	Talent Agent	28
3	Voice Talent	36
4	Stuntperson	44
5	The Extra	52
6	Writer	58
7	Production Assistant	66
8	Script Supervisor	71
9	Location Scout	80
10	The Grip	88
11	The Gaffer	92
12	Wardrobe	96
13	The Makeup Artist	103
14	Special Effects Artist	108
15	Animator	114
16	Foley Artist	119
17	Puppeteer	125
18	Other Careers	132
	Glossary	137
	Index	140

INTRODUCTION

Congratulations. You have just picked up a book that may help you to decide what to do with the rest of your life. You have decided to forego a college education, at least for now, and you have realized that you have to go to work. Drawing upon your skills and interests of the last few years, you have picked up this book to see what types of careers you might find in the film and television industry.

The opportunities are vast, ranging from acting to makeup to working as an electrician. In fact, there are so many avenues you might pursue within the broad field of film and television that all the possibilities cannot possibly be covered in a book this size. However, by reading this book you will get a generous sampling of the opportunities out there. You will also get advice on how to pursue various careers in the industry. One important thing to understand is that while there are many careers available in the industry, you cannot just walk in and expect to be hired. Most of the careers within the television and film industry require hard work and a lot of dedication, not to mention working for little or no money before you reach your goal. This is an industry in which, unless you are one of the extremely lucky ones, you will find it necessary to pay your dues, so to speak, before you make it to the big time.

At the end of each chapter you will find a directory. It would be nice if everything you need to know to work in a particular career could be found in each directory, but the fact of the matter is that each career's directory could easily encompass a full-sized book in and of itself. In fact, many such books exist and some will be mentioned throughout this book. It is in no way possible for this book to give you all the tools you need to launch a successful career in the film or television industry. It is possible, however, for you to get an idea of what to do, how to do it, and where to go for further guidance. Therefore, what you will find in each directory is a sampling of things you might look to in order to find work in that career field. This information will supplement the information within each chapter. However, in an industry such as film and television, where so many people do so many things, and where the competition is so tough, it will be up to you to prove your desire to work by going out and finding all of the resources that you need. Just remember what almost anyone working in this fascinating industry will tell you: "No one is going to hand this work to you. If you want it, you must go after it with everything you've got."

This book is filled with career ideas that might interest you if you think you would like to work either in front of the camera or behind the scenes in the film and television industry. While you still may not know exactly what you want to do, at the very least this book will give you some tools to work with that will help you do further research and discover what you might want to do with your life. You will find that many of the career suggestions in this book depend on your having a certain type of personality. You will have to be strong, self-motivated, and willing to work very hard for what you want. The competition in the film and television industry is tough. If you think you have what it takes, then the good news is that you probably do!

Before you get started, there is one important question that you must ask yourself: "Where do I live?" If you are currently living in Chicago, New York, or Los Angeles, you are living right in the heart of the biggest television and film production centers in the country. These cities have the most opportunities, the greatest resources, and the most stuff actually going on. If you live in a smaller city such as St. Louis, Dallas, Minneapolis, Milwaukee, or Miami, you will still find trade papers, classes, good photographers, and career opportunities. If you live in a town with a name like Duluth, Rockford, Elk Cove, Decatur, or Rock Falls, on the other hand, you will have to consider whether or not you are willing to relocate to find the career of your dreams. If you are not willing to move out of your small town and take up residence in one of the big cities, you might want to rethink this whole film and television career thing. After all, you simply cannot get a job where no job exists. However, if you are serious and you are willing to relocate, read this book and then get packing!

1

ACTOR

The most obvious choice that comes to mind when you are thinking about a career in the film or television industry is that of an actor. An actor is a person who entertains people by pretending to be a character in a television show, movie, play, or commercial. Just about anyone can become a film or television actor, and certainly you do not need a college degree to become one. It can be a long, difficult road to success. If you love drama club or star in every high school play possible, or if you simply love to be the center of attention, a career in acting may be just the career for you. You will have to be strong and bold and willing to go out and make yourself known. A career as an actor is not a good career for the shy, the timid, or those whose feelings are easily hurt. To be an actor, you need to have a great deal of confidence in yourself.

Getting Started

Your first step is going to be to find a regular pay-the-bills job. Your best bet will be to sign up with a temporary employment agency or wait tables at a restaurant. You will need to find a job with a flexible schedule that will work around your demanding schedule as an actor. It is the nature of the acting profession that work is often sporadic and that many actors spend a good deal of time unemployed as actors. You will still have to pay the rent and bills.

Training

Even if you were in every single play that your high school produced in the last four years, some professional training will not hurt. In addition to helping you perfect your skills, taking some acting, movement, or voice classes can help

Many would-be actors work as waiters to pay their living expenses while they wait for their "big break."

put you in touch with the people who cast the television and film productions you hope to be in. Several major acting schools are listed in this chapter's directory. Your local phone book is a good source to locate acting classes in your area. Check to see if your city has a bookstore specifically for actors and others in the field. This bookstore will be a good source for notices of local auditions and classes to take. Find out who teaches the classes. You will want to know if the teacher is someone well known in the industry or someone who is just teaching out of the need to make a buck. Find out if any successful actors have come out of the training center. Ask about the levels of classes the school offers. If you have absolutely no experience whatsoever, you will benefit from a class in the basics of acting before you move up to more advanced classes. A more seasoned actor who already has some experience under his or her belt may prefer to start higher up, perhaps in an intermediate or advanced acting class.

As long as you are checking out acting classes, you may also want to look into some of the other classes that may help you move your acting career along. Places to look for these classes are your local phone book, the Internet, or the theater division of your local university or community college.

Photography

Actors need photographers. They need to maintain picture portfolios that present themselves attractively to potential employers. One of the pictures you will need is a head shot. A head shot is an 8" x 10" black-and-white photograph of your head and face. This photo will become your calling card. It is often the first image that the people who hire actors for movies, television shows, and commercials will see of you. Because your photographs may be looked at before you are actually seen in person, it is crucial that you have an excellent, flattering head shot that also looks like you.

A producer's assistant sorts photos and identification forms for prospective extras during a casting call.

The head shot must be taken by a professional photographer who specializes in photographing actors. You can find the name of a good photographer back at that bookstore, or in one of the actors' trade journals like *Variety* or *Billboard*. Do not skimp or try to save money when you are getting your head shot done. Good head shots can be expensive, especially if you are having them taken by a well-known photographer. Spend the money. A good head shot may mean the difference between getting work and not getting work. A reputable photographer should allow you to stop by his or her studio to have a look at the work he or she has done. This is a courtesy and should not cost you any money. If the photographer asks for money, cancel your appointment and look for another photographer. No money should change hands until you actually have an appointment set up to have your photos taken.

Find out how much the photographer charges for each roll of film he or she shoots. Then ask, on average, how many rolls of film are shot in a session. You'll want to know how many actual photos you will get. It's important to know what to wear, whether or not you should do your own hair and makeup, or whether the photographer has someone in the studio to do these for you. Ask if the photographer guarantees his or her work. If you get your proofsheet back and you do not like any of the shots, will the photographer reshoot for a nominal fee, or only if there is an obvious error in the lighting or the focus? Any good photographer should guarantee his or her work. Head shots are too important; you need to have the best.

"Make sure your head shot stands out," says Sandy Watson, an actor, director, and producer in Los Angeles. "And not because it is a stunt shot, like you posed half naked or something. It should stand out because there is a special glimmer in your eyes that makes the person looking at it wonder what you are thinking about. That is the best shot."

Once you have chosen the photo you feel best represents you, you will need to have it reproduced. Ask your photographer if he or she can recommend a printer. To start out, have about 100 to 200 head shots made, with your name printed along the bottom. Having more made later will never be as expensive as this first time.

The Résumé

As with any type of career search, you will need to put together a résumé. The actor's résumé will be somewhat different from your typical job résumé. It will tell more about who you are than any other type of résumé would. If you are just getting started in your acting career, chances are you will not have much to put on your résumé. Nonetheless, you need one.

Your first résumé will be sparse. It will start with your name, in big, bold letters right at the top. You will need to include your basic statistics: height, weight, eye color, and hair color. Do not lie. If you are caught misrepresenting yourself, it could damage your reputation as a serious actor. Lying could also put you in a tight spot, as you may be expected to do something that you really cannot do. Remember when Matt LeBlanc's character, Joey, on the situation comedy *Friends* lied on his résumé? His résumé said that he had all sorts of dance training when in fact he was a total octopus on the dance floor. He blew an important audition when the dance captain assumed Joey could teach the dance combination when he actually could not.

On your résumé you will include any experience that you have, such as the high school plays you were in. You will also want to list the classes that you have taken or are taking. At the bottom of your résumé, list any special skills you may have, such as tap dancing, singing, figure skating, basketball, yodeling, juggling, baton twirling, or whatever you are good at that might help you land an acting job. List anything you can do, no matter how bizarre it is.

Eventually, as you begin to do some professional acting, you will be able to eliminate all of your high school and summer camp productions from your résumé. In the meantime, they count as real experience. One thing you do NOT want to include on your résumé is the date of the work. Do not include *when* you did any of your work. The fact that you did the work is enough. Also, do not include your age on your résumé. It is against the law for an agent or director to ask your age, except to ask if you are indeed over eighteen. They can ask what your age range is, or what age you play, but they cannot ask your actual age. Besides, in the eyes of the camera, the casting director, and the agent, you are as

old as you look. Let the people seeking to hire you decide how old you are.

Never put your home address on your résumé. Often, head shots get thrown away and anyone can find them. The finder not only has your contact information, but a really good photo of what you look like. You must also reduce your résumé to a size no more than 8" x 10" so that it fits neatly on the back of your head shot. Never go anywhere without at least a few copies of your head shot and résumé. You never know whom you might meet and you always want to be prepared.

"As a general rule, do not list work you do as an extra on your résumé unless you are truly a featured extra. Casting directors dislike it when you list extra work. Use extra work for experience and contacts, but not for résumé filler," says Sandy Watson.

The Agent

You will need to list with a talent agent to get work as an actor. Not every agent out there will be interested in representing you. If you live in Chicago, seek representation from as many agencies as you can. This is called multi-listing. Please note that you can only multi-list in Chicago. You will get blacklisted (marked for exclusion from work) if you try to do this in either Los Angeles or New York.

Keep Working!

While you are hoping to land that great role in a film or on television, keep up your acting skills by auditioning for and playing roles in stage plays. Not only will you always be busy and have new things to put on your résumé, you just never know who might be sitting in the audience one night! It could be a famous casting director, an agent, or a producer. Hard work and persistence are the keys to making it big in this industry. You may hear of someone in the business referred to as a newcomer. Rest assured, this newcomer did not just walk into a Hollywood studio and say, "Hi, put me in a movie." More often than not this actor has been paying his or her dues for years, modeling for print ads, doing television commercials, or taking small walk-on roles in television specials.

Acting can be one of the toughest film and television fields to break into. If it is what you want to do, however, do not give up. Continue to wait on tables or work for the temp agency. Be persistent with the agents. Remember, however, that there is a difference between being persistent and being obnoxious. One will help you get work, the other will not.

Associations

In the field of film and television, the associations you will look for are the unions. There are two main unions: AFTRA (American Federation of Television and Radio Artists) and SAG (Screen Actors Guild). According to *Act One Reports*, the "primary responsibilities of the unions include: negotiating contracts that establish the minimum wage scale and working conditions for professional performers; enforcement of those contracts; processing residuals; regulation and franchising of talent agencies; membership record keeping and communications."

Chicago, Los Angeles, and New York all have union offices that you can contact, as do some of the smaller cities, such as Cleveland, Dallas, Denver, Nashville, Philadelphia, Phoenix, Pittsburgh, San Diego, San Francisco, and Seattle. You can go to http://www.aftra.com for more AFTRA information. You can learn about AFTRA's local publications, *Cleveland aftranow*, *Los Angeles Diallog*, *New York StandBy*, *Pittsburgh aftranewsbriefs*, and *San Francisco Open Mike,* at http://www.aftra.com/resources/publications.html.

Networking

Talk, listen, network. The best information you can gather will be from fellow actors or other people working in the film and television business. Talk to your acting teacher, your classmates in acting school, your photographer, the people at the bookstores, and other people you run into at agencies and auditions. This business is really all about networking and being in the right place at the right time!

Pay

It is hard to give a pay scale for this industry. As you may well know, television actors like Jerry Seinfeld, the cast of *ER*, the cast of *Friends*, and so many others, not to mention film actors such as Tom Hanks, Julia Roberts, and John Travolta, can pull in millions of dollars per television episode or motion picture. You hear about these actors and their contract negotiations in the news all the time. It seems like an outrageous amount of money for simply doing a job. But it is the reality of the business. There is no way to predict accurately how much money you can make working in front of the camera in the film and television industry. An extra can make $100 a day. So it is safe to say that the pay range runs from $100 a day to $1 million per episode to millions of dollars per film.

FOR MORE INFORMATION

ACTING STUDIOS

Piven Theatre Workshop
927 Noyes
Evanston, IL 60201
(847) 866-6597

TVI Actors Studio
California: (818) 784-6500
New York: (212) 302-1900
(800) TVI-2772

BOOKS

Buzzell, Linda. *How to Make It in Hollywood*. New York: Harperperennial Library, 1996.
Whether you're an aspiring actor, writer, director, designer, agent, or studio executive, this book tells you everything you need to know about agents, managers, lawyers, the casting couch, handling rejection, how to be lucky, and all the steps you need to achieve success.

Farris, Linda Guess. *Television Careers: A Guide to Breaking and Entering*. Los Angeles: Buy the Book Enterprises, 1995.

Peterson, Linda. *Careers Without College*. Princeton, NJ: Peterson's, 1994.

The map that you must have in Los Angeles is called *The Thomas Guide*. Agents even give you directions by saying things like, "You are going to Danny Goldman Casting. That's on page 369 of *The Thomas Guide.*"

BOOKSTORES

Act I
2540 N. Lincoln
Chicago, IL 60614
(800) 55-PLAYS (557-5297)
Web site: http://www.act1books.com

Samuel French, Inc.
7623 Sunset Boulevard, Dept.W
Hollywood, CA 90046
(323) 876-0570

Samuel French, Inc.
45 West 25th Street, Dept.W
New York, NY 10010
(212) 206-8990

WEB SITES

The Academy Players Directory Link
http://www.breakdownservices.com

Act One Resource Center
http://www.actone.com
This Web site has examples of photographers' work, audition notices, and more.

Backstage
http://www.backstage.com
This is a New York–based and West Coast Web site that features national and regional theater coverage.

PerformInk
http://www.performink.com
This Web site tells you more about what is going on in Chicago.

Samuel French
http://www.samuelfrench.com

This site will give you all the information you need about Samuel French, the bookseller specializing in plays and scripts. You can also order the Samuel French Catalog, which lists plays, monologues, audition material, classroom guides, and classic works.

The Tory Christopher Group Talent Agency
http://www.tcg-2000.com

TRADE PUBLICATIONS

Each large city has its own publications. Write or call the publication offices for subscription information if you are not currently living in a big city. Quite often these trade publications are free, or can be subscribed to for a nominal fee.

Backstage
1515 Broadway, 14th Floor
New York, NY 10036
(212) 764-7300
Backstage is a publication out of New York that features national and regional theater coverage.

Backstage West
5055 Wilshire Boulevard, 5th Floor
Los Angeles, CA 90036
(323) 525-2356
Backstage West is Backstage's West Coast counterpart. Another publication worth looking into if you are planning to work in Los Angeles.

PerformInk
3223 N. Sheffield, 3rd Floor
Chicago, IL 60657-2210
(773) 296-4600
Chicago's *PerformInk* comes out once a week, chock full of great information about theater and the film trade in Chicago. If you live in Chicago you can get this paper for free.

Ross Reports Television and Film
1515 Broadway, 14th Floor
New York, NY 10036
(800) 817-3273
Ross Reports Television and Film is a monthly publication that focuses on agents, casting directors, and film and television in both New York and Los Angeles. *Ross Reports* also publishes annually *The USA Talent Directory*, which is a national guide of available talent for agents and casting directors.

Variety
P.O. Box 15878
North Hollywood, CA 91615-5878
(800) 323-4345
Variety focuses mainly on what is happening in Los Angeles and New York.

The Working Actor's Guide
Aaron Blake Publishers
15608 S. New Century Drive
Gardena, CA 90248
(310) 965-0290

PHOTOGRAPHERS

David Beeler
2054 Argyle Avenue
Los Angeles, CA 90068-3361
(323) 464-4728

David Beyda Studio
140 W. 32nd Street, 2nd Floor
New York, NY 10001
(212) 967-6964
Web site: http://www.davidbeyda.com

Jennifer Girard
1455 West Roscoe
Chicago, IL 60657
(773) 929-3730

Kelsey Edwards Photography
633 North La Brea Avenue, 2nd Floor
Los Angeles, CA 90036
(323) 936-6106

Lesley Bohm Photography
201 South Santa Fe Avenue, Suite 301
Los Angeles, CA 90012
(213) 625-8401

Suzanne Plunkett
2047 N. Lincoln, Suite 300
Chicago, IL 60657
(773) 477-3775

Tom Lascher
1635 Electric Avenue
Venice, CA 90291-4803
(310) 581-1980

2

TALENT AGENT

Talent agents are the people who get work for actors. They are the actors' friends, though to talk to actors you might never know it. Actors may say that agents can often be abrupt or seem uninterested in them. This is simply because they are very busy people doing a lot of things at once. Talent agents work with casting directors, actors, and, in the case of commercials, advertising agencies and sponsors. It is up to the talent agent to go through the massive files in his or her office and choose the résumés and photographs of actors that he or she believes would suit the client's needs. For example, the client may be doing a commercial for a new car. He is looking for a young woman to talk about why this car is the best and most exciting new car out there. The talent agent must choose head shots carefully, finding young women who look like they would be driving this type of fun, new car. She must choose women within a certain age range, and also with a certain look, as specified by the client. Then the agent calls all of the actors and books them for the upcoming audition. She may or may not sit in on the audition process, assisting the client or casting director in making a decision regarding whom to hire.

Basically, then, it is the talent agent's job to represent actors and recommend them for roles. As a talent agent, you will need to have a good memory for names and faces. You will have to remember details about the actors you represent. When an actor calls to check in and ask if you have any work for him, you will need to have an idea who this actor is, what his age range is, and what he looks like. This is a career for someone who works well under pressure. You will often have a very short period of time in which to choose the actors you wish to send out on an audition.

A good talent agent works hard for his or her actors, getting them frequent auditions for interesting and well-paying roles. Legitimate talent agents do not ask for money from actors up front. No legitimate agent makes his or her money by taking it from an actor before getting the actor work. Agents make their money by taking a 10 to 20 percent agent fee off the top of any paychecks that their actors receive.

Different talent agencies represent different types of actors. For example, in Chicago there are about twenty-six talent agencies, twenty of which represent union members (that is, actors who are members of SAG or AFTRA), and five or six agencies represent nonunion actors. These are actors who are either new to the business or who have not yet done enough work to become eligible for union membership. Within a given talent agency, you may have any number of agents who specialize in different areas of radio, film, television, and live performance. A larger talent agency may have individual agents who represent children, teens, men, or women. One agent may specialize in on-camera performers, whereas another specializes in print models or voice-over talent. There may be one agent who handles all the new actors just getting started in the business.

Talent agents spend a lot of time on the telephone trying to match their clients with studios.

Most talent agencies set aside one day each week when new talent can come by and register. The actor brings his résumé and head shot. As a talent agent, it will be your responsibility to assess each actor and decide if you want to represent that person. You cannot survive for very long as a talent agent if you send out actors who are not very good. Evaluating actors is a skill that comes with experience. You can gain experience by attending auditions organized by producers and casting agents or occasionally other talent agents. You will also attend the theater quite a bit, studying performances and looking out for talented actors who are not yet represented.

As you gain experience, you will find yourself becoming more and more of an intimate advisor and perhaps even a parent figure to some of the actors you represent. You will find yourself telling actors what to wear to auditions, how to restyle their hair or makeup, or how to present themselves. Working as a talent agent can be a very rewarding career. It is also a lot of work, and you must be willing to go that extra mile for your clients. You will have to learn how to negotiate contracts for actors, and how to get the most money and best terms. You will be responsible for following up and ensuring that your clients get paid.

Training

There is no specific training program for becoming a talent agent. Many of today's talent agents start out as actors. For one reason or another, they have chosen to give up acting and concentrate on agenting. You may like the idea of putting talented people to work. Start out as the front desk receptionist or an office clerk for a talent agent. Learn the ropes of the business and you could end up with a talent agency with your own name on it in a few years.

FOR MORE INFORMATION

For more information about a career as a talent agent, contact any of the agents found in:

Act One Reports
640 N. LaSalle, Suite 535
Chicago, IL 60610-3731
(312) 787-9384
e-mail: actone@actone.com
Web site: http://www.actone.com

Casting by McLean
P.O. Box 10569
Chicago, IL 60610

KTs
P.O. Box 577039
Chicago, IL 60657

WEB SITES

AKA Talent Agency
http://www.akatalent.com

Breakdown Service
http://www.breakdownservices.com

Buzz NYC/Buzz LA
http://www.buzznyc.com

Castnet.com
http://www.castnet.com

Future Casting 2000
http://www.futurecasting2000.com

Future Casting Job Site
http://www.futurecasting2000.com/job_listings.htm

Hollywood Access Directory
http://www.hollydex.com

NYC FAME
http://www.nycfame.com/generalsite/talentagenthotline.htm

Online Talent Agency
http://www.onlinetalent.com

BOOKS

Biederman, Donald E. *Law and Business of the Entertainment Industries*. Fourth edition. New York: Praeger Publishing, 2001.

Litwak, Mark. *Contracts for the Film & Television Industry*. Los Angeles: Silman-James, 1999.

Members Only Guide to American Model and Talent Agencies. New York: Federation of Actors, Models and Entertainers, 2000. Available exclusively from the NYC Fame store: http://www.nycfame.com/store.

Moore, Schuyler M. *The Biz: The Basic Business, Legal and Financial Aspects of the Film Industry*. Los Angeles: Silman-James, 2000.

Orenstein, Harold, and David E. Guinn. *Entertainment Law and Business: A Guide to the Law and Business Practices of the Entertainment Industry*. Carlsbad, CA: Michie Publishing, 1989.

Resnik, Gail. *All You Need to Know About the Movie and TV Business*. New York: Fireside, 1996.

TRADE PUBLICATIONS

Association of Talent Agents Newsletter
9255 Sunset Boulevard, #318
Los Angeles, CA 90069
(213) 274-0628

3

VOICE TALENT

You love to speak in different voices. You are great at accents and dialects. You do a terrific George W. Bush impression. Perhaps your career is in voice work. Voice talents are the people whose off-screen voices lend that special something to television shows, films, and commercials to make them truly entertaining. The work you can do as voice talent is broad. Full-length animated films use voice talent to speak the parts of the animated characters seen on screen. Some television shows, such as the 1990s hit *The Wonder Years*, and many films use a narrator. A narrator is someone whose voice is heard off-screen telling the viewer more specific details of the story.

The next time you watch television, pay some attention to the commercials. Notice that almost every commercial has a narrator—that is, a person who talks about the product but whom you cannot see. This is a different person from the actors in the commercial. This is a person who does voice-overs for a living.

Voice Tapes

If you want to pursue a career in voice work, you will need a professional voice tape. This is a regular cassette tape with samples of your voice doing different things, such as speaking with different accents, narrating part of a story, and reading commercials, all set to music. Your voice tape should be only about two minutes long. The voice tape has to be made in a studio. Before you go in to make your voice tape, you will need to know specifically what to put on it.

Agents

Talent agents are the people who will get you voice work. You will need to find out which agents in your area represent voice talent. Get to know your agents. Let them hear your voice. Remember, these people are very busy and may seem to be in a hurry. Do not be a pest, but let your self-confidence step forward. Be strong. Assert yourself. Be persistent. Check in as frequently as you are allowed to. Talent agents do not ask for money up front to get you work. If an agent asks for money from you, walk away. Do expect the agent to take a 10 percent to 20 percent agent fee off the top of any paychecks you receive.

Although you are hoping to pursue your voice talent career in television and film, you may at first find that your agent is booking you for radio work, for something like commercials. At the beginning, when you are just getting started, you will want to take whatever work your agent offers you. These smaller jobs will give your voice plenty of exposure. They help you to gain the experience you need. They will help to build your reputation as a reliable, easy to work with voice talent and, just as important, they will pay you well!

> Dionne Quan, who is blind, reads a script translated into braille as she practices the voice of Kimi from the *Rugrats* cartoon. She is the voice of Kimi in both the movie and the television series.

Training

It is recommended that you take a class in voice-overs to get a handle on how all this works. Your city should have an acting studio that teaches a class in voice work. Most cities have schools that offer all sorts of different classes, from ballroom dancing and pottery to computer basics and foreign languages. These centers usually have some classes that cover film and television careers, and you are likely to find a voice-over class there as well. Wherever you find it, take this class. Your teacher will not only tell you what you need to know to make the voice tape itself, but you will also find out where and how much it will cost to make the voice tape. The teacher will also give you guidelines as to how many copies of the voice tape you will need to have made, how to create a catchy cover (called a j-card) for your voice tape, and to whom you should deliver your voice tapes once they are ready.

You may also want to take some classes in diction. These classes will help ensure that you are able to speak clearly and at the right pace so that you are easily understood. A singing class does not hurt either. And although you may have already decided that you do not want to act on screen, it is important to understand that even though only your voice may be featured, you are still acting! There is a big difference between simply reading lines and actually acting them so that what you are saying is believable. This is why you are called "voice *talent*" and not just "voice." So take one or two basic acting classes, just so that you can sound like you really mean it when you tell your listeners to buy Super Sweet Smelling Soap or if you land your big break doing the voice for a new Disney character in a feature-length animated film.

FOR MORE INFORMATION

VOICE-OVER CLASSES
The Discovery Center
2940 N. Lincoln Avenue
Chicago, IL 60657
(773) 348-8120

IN NEW YORK
David Zema, Voice of Success Programs
122 West 26th Street, 2nd Floor
New York, NY 10010
(212) 473-6448
Web site: http://www.davidzema.com

TJ's Voices
Classes & Demo Tapes
(212) 465-8050

IN CALIFORNIA
Nova Productions
3575 Cahuenga Boulevard West, 2nd Floor
Los Angeles, CA 90068
(323) 969-0949

Rick Zieff's Unbelievably Fun Voice-Over Class
(323) 651-1666

The Voice Factory
81 Lansing Street, Suite 207
San Francisco, CA 94105
Web site: http://www.thevoicefactory.com

Voice Over
1119 Mission Street
San Francisco, CA 94103-1514
(415) 626-1386
Web site: http://www.voiceonline.com/classes/onedayclasses.html

VOICE-OVER DEMO TAPE PRODUCTION

Audio One Studio
325 W. Huron, Suite 512
Chicago, IL 60610

Sound Advice
2028 W. Potomac, Suite 2
Chicago, IL 60622
Web site: http://www.voiceoverinfo.com

WEB SITES

Sound Advice
http://www.voiceoverinfo.com

Voices On
e-mail: tomtest@prodigy.net

BOOKS

Apple, Terri. *Making Money in Voice-Overs*. Los Angeles: Lone Eagle Publishing Company, 1999.

Blu, Susan, and Molly Ann Mullin. *Word of Mouth*. Los Angeles: Pomegranate Press, Ltd., 1999.

Shaw, Bernard Graham. *Voice Overs: A Practical Guide*. New York: Routledge, 2000.

4

STUNTPERSON

They jump out of airplanes. They drive like maniacs through city streets. They scale large buildings. They fight to the death with the arch-enemies of humankind. They are the specialists called stuntpeople. They perform these acts of bravery so that actors can remain safe and do their jobs as actors. If you have been taking gymnastics for years or are great at dance or a certain sport, if you are in excellent physical condition, if you are not afraid of taking chances, if you love to drive fast, or if acting is really not your thing, you might consider the high-risk career of a stuntperson.

Toward the end of the credits of almost any movie you watch, you will find that stunt players were used, possibly without your even realizing that the film had stunts. A stuntperson's role in a film can be something as basic as riding a horse off into the sunset or performing a dance sequence that an actor is incapable of performing for himself or herself. Or the job might be to go through the moves of an elaborate fight scene or climb the side of a skyscraper. Often, brave actors do their own stunts, but even more often they choose to avoid dangerous situations that could harm them physically, thus ruining their careers.

As a stuntperson, you will need head shots and full-body shots accompanied by a résumé listing your skills and previous credits. Read the chapter about actors to find out all about how to get head shots taken and how to put together a good résumé. Often, stuntpeople will start their own Web sites that talent agents can access. Credits, photos, and even video clips can be displayed on your Web site. Some stuntpeople's Web sites are listed at the end of this chapter.

Many stuntpeople are hired not only because of their skills and their reputations, but also because they look like the actors they will be portraying during the stunt. This does not mean that you have to be a dead-ringer for Tom Cruise in order to be hired to do stunts for him. Your face is not likely to be shown on screen while you are performing as a stuntperson. However, it will be necessary for you to have roughly the same color hair and physical build, and of course you will need to be the same gender. You will probably join a union (SAG), and you can even list yourself in directories of stuntpeople. You never know what actor may need you to be his or her stunt double!

Training

It is vital that you have training to be a stuntperson. You cannot simply say one day, "Hey, I think I will become a stuntperson," and then just walk in and get a job. This would be a very dangerous way to approach this type of career. You absolutely must have training. There is a special exception to this rule, however. If you already have a background in which you have used your body to perform some strenuous

Stuntman and country singer Billy Dean performs a stunt fall through a window while filming a scene for a music video.

Stage combat class is a good way to gain experience as a stuntperson.

or dangerous physical activity, you may not need further extensive stunt training. Such a special background would involve some activity that really tests your body's strength, stamina, and ability. Some good examples are gymnastics, wrestling, and circus experience. You may also use other talents that you have, such as skiing, race car driving, piloting a plane, dancing, and activities of this nature, to get work as a stuntperson. Many stuntpeople started out as actors but find that they prefer the thrill of doing their own stunts so much that they decide to perform stunts as a career.

It is very important to remember that unless you have extensive experience in some such activity, you must have proper stunt training so that you can safely perform the dangerous stunts that the script requires. In the directory at the end of this chapter, you will find a few training schools. You have to learn to use your body properly. You should learn how to drive safely so that you can perform high-speed chases for movies. Special schools teach these things, and it is important that you take these courses to ensure your own safety.

FOR MORE INFORMATION

ORGANIZATIONS

Bobby Ore Motorsports
P.O. Box 8794
Calabasas, CA 91372
(818) 880-5678
Web site: http://www.bobbyoresports.com

League of Independent Stunt Players
P.O. Box 196
Madison Square Garden
New York, NY 10159
(212) 777-7021

Stunt Contact
553 N. Pacific Coast Highway #248
Redondo Beach, CA 90277
(310) 540-5571
(800) 707-8868
Web site: http://www.stuntcontact.com
List yourself as a stuntperson and get more information about the industry.

Stuntmen's Association of Motion Pictures, Inc.
10660 Riverside Drive
2nd Floor East, Suite E
Toluca, CA 91602
(818) 766-4334
Web site: http://www.stuntmen.com

WEB SITES

Alliance for Stunt Performers of Color
http://www.africana.com/key/alliance_for_stunt_performers_of_color.htm

Light Speed Entertainment
http://crazykamikaze.com/

SAG Online Stunt Performers Guide
http://www.sag.org/stuntperformer.html

Stuntmen's Association
http://www.stuntmen.com

StuntNet: The Internet Resource for Stunts
http://www.stuntnet.com

StuntPerformers.com
http://www.stuntperformers.com

Stunt Person Directory
http://hollywood-911.com

Stuntplayers Directory
http://www.stuntplayer.com

Stunts Canada
http://www.stuntscanada.net

United Stuntwomen's Association
http://www.usastunt.com

BOOKS

Frese, Gene Scott. *Hollywood Stunt Performers*. Jefferson, NC: McFarland & Co, 1998.

Ireland, Karin. *Hollywood Stuntpeople*. New York: J. Messner, 1980.

Resnik, Gail, and Scott Trost. *All You Need to Know About the Movie and TV Business*. New York: Fireside, 1996.

Ware, Derek. *Stunt Performers*. Ada, OK: Garrett Educational Corporation, 1992.

5

THE EXTRA

An extra is someone who works in film and television as part of the crowd. Believe it or not, many people make full careers for themselves doing extra work. Extras are a very important part of the film and television industry because they make the film or television show appear more real, or more lifelike. Turn on your television and you will see extras in almost every scene of every television show and commercial. See those guys in the back enjoying their burgers and chatting with the cute girl who just walked by? See how they just sort of fill in the shot? They create movement. They create life. They almost never have lines, their names are not listed in the credits, and the viewer knows virtually nothing about their characters. So, why would anyone want to become an extra?

Extras get to be on television and in the movies, yet they are not burdened with having to learn lines. They often get a decent paycheck for the work they do, they get exposure in the field, and they get a good deal of experience learning the ropes of working in the film and television industry. Many actors use extra work as a way to earn supplemental income, get to know other actors, and gain exposure with directors and casting directors. Many an actor first got his or her feet wet in the industry by doing extra work. In California, extras even had their own union, the Screen Extras Guild. That's right, the extra industry is so big in Los Angeles that for some people this is a complete line of work. In other words, these people make a career for themselves working as extras. Today, the Screen Actors Guild (SAG) covers union extras. SAG extras are entitled to vouchers for mileage, overtime pay, and the same on-set meals that the actors get to eat.

Would-be extras fill out forms in response to a casting call.

One of the most exciting things about working as an extra is that you may have a chance to meet some famous people. Movies and even some television shows are being shot on location all over the country nowadays. This means that a production company could just pop into your town, no matter where you live, and film scenes for an upcoming movie. When this happens, the production company counts on the locals to fill in as extras. Open calls for extras are most often announced on local radio stations or in local newspapers. Sometimes the production company holds

auditions, but more often they simply ask people to show up at a certain time and place dressed in a certain style of clothing. Unfortunately, these gigs do not always pay, but once again, they give you experience, exposure, and networking opportunities, and they are a good place to get started in your television or film acting career.

You should register with an extras casting company if you want to do work as an extra. Extras casting companies are responsible for hiring certain people to make the film look just right. As an extra, expect long hours and a lot of sitting around waiting to shoot the scene. On the upside, this is a great way to get your foot in the door, so do not rule it out until you have tried it.

FOR MORE INFORMATION

EXTRA CASTING AGENCIES

Casting by McLean
P.O. Box 10569
Chicago, IL 60610
(Do not call.)

Central Casting
220 South Flower Street
Burbank, CA 91502
(818) 562-2755

Holzer & Ridge Casting
(773) 549-3169

KT's
P.O. Box 577039
Chicago, IL 60657

WEB SITES

Castnet Extras
http://www.castnetextras.com

EntertainmentCareers.net
http://www.entertainmentcareers.net

Extra Cast
http://www.extracast.com

GetGigs.com: Film Extras
http://www.getgigs.com

The Global Movie Extras Network
http://www.gmxgroup.com/

Hollywoodweb
http://www.hollywoodweb.com
Internet casting service for actors, extras, models, and technicians.
Find out about free registration, or visit the job bulletin board.

Movie Extras Registration and Resources
http://www.moviex.com

BOOKS

Chambers, Cullen. *The Complete Back to One Movie Extras Guide Book, The Millennium Edition*. Hollywood, CA: Back To One, 2000.

Movie Extras Guidebook: How to Make Good Money as a Background Actor in Film and TV. Hollywood, CA: Back to One, 1996.

Resnik, Gail, and Scott Trost. *All You Need to Know About the Movie and TV Business*. New York: Fireside, 1996.

6

WRITER

Have you ever sat in front of your television set and thought to yourself, "I could write a better sitcom than that!" If you love to write or you have really creative, cool ideas, why not put them down on paper? Although plenty of people think they have next year's Oscar-winning script ready to jot down on the printed page, it only takes one good script to win.

As a scriptwriter, your number-one responsibility is to tell a story. The writer works closely not only with the film or television show's director, but also with other writers to develop the story and the screenplay or script. Initially you will do most of your work wherever you feel you write the best: at home sitting at your computer, under a tree at the park, in the café of your favorite bookstore. In other words, first you have to do your writing. If you want your script to be taken seriously, consider enrolling in a course on script-writing, check out some books on the subject, and study what several Web sites in this chapter's directory have to say on the matter. You will want to be sure that you are using the correct terminology when you are writing directions for your screenplay. Furthermore, most studios will not even read your script if it is not formatted properly. It must conform to certain guidelines. Look at the formatting program listed in the directory that follows for help in getting your screenplay to look just right. After you have put your fabulous ideas on paper, submit them to the various movie and television studios. You never know. Your idea may be the next big movie or television show!

You have to know how to submit a completed screenplay. Here are the basics. For feature-length motion pictures, the screenplay must be typed in a standard format of about 90 to 110 typed pages. Obviously some features run longer or shorter, so this is just an average to keep in mind when

you are writing. If you are writing a script for a low-budget film, you should limit it to about ninety pages.

Lines for actors are typed within the center section of the page. Always use a computer word-processing program to type your script. With the number of revisions your script is likely to undergo, you will want the ability to make changes easily and quickly. Type in a standard font, nothing fancy. Use a normal 12-point type and be sure your paper is standard 8-1/2" x 11" letter size paper. This makes for a familiar blueprint for the director to use.

Once a studio has accepted your idea and begins to turn your screenplay into an actual movie or television show, you may have to spend a lot of time at the studio working on revisions. This will be to your benefit, actually, because you will want to protect the integrity of your script. In other words, if a revision or a change needs to be made, you want to be the one to make it. After all, this is your screenplay. You must realize, however, that a script for a movie or television show is a collaborative effort, and that producers, directors, actors, and even sponsors may request changes.

A screenwriter works on a new script on his laptop computer.

The writer must be able to write and deliver the script on time. No matter how good a writer you are, if you cannot make your deadlines, someone who can meet deadlines will replace you. After you have delivered your screenplay, it will remain your responsibility to do any necessary rewrites and polish the script.

Another great way to put your writing talent to work is as a studio writer. Rather than submit new scripts to a film or television production company, you will be a regular employee of such a company and will revise the scripts of others. You may produce original scripts in collaboration with members of a writing team for a weekly television show.

Training

You may really enjoy writing, but do you know how to write a screenplay? Your local community college may provide classes in different types of writing. Enroll in one of these classes. Your best bet is a class in playwriting or screenwriting. You will study the specifics of how to do this type of writing. You will learn where and how to submit your work, how much money to expect your work to bring in, and what organizations you may want to join for support, critiques, and more advice.

FOR MORE INFORMATION

ASSOCIATIONS

Screenwriters Group
P.O. Box 255
Palatine, IL 60078
(847) 859-7483

SCHOOLS

Center Theatre Ensemble's Training Center
1346 W. Devon
Chicago, IL 60660
(773) 508-0200

Chicago Dramatists Workshop
1105 W. Chicago
Chicago, IL 60622
(312) 633-0630

WEB SITES

All of these Web sites will help you find more books and information about starting a career as a screenwriter.

Filmtracker Infosource
http://www.filmtracker.com

Hollywood Creative Directory
http://www.hcdonline.com

Hollywood Reporter
http://www.hollywoodreporter.com

In Hollywood
http://www.inhollywood.com

Screenwriters Utopia
http://www.screenwritersutopia.com
This is an especially good site for screenwriters with little or no experience.

TV Writers
http://www.tvwriter.com
A comprehensive list of TV writing information.

Variety
http://www.variety.com

Writers Guild of America
http://www.wga.org

BOOKS

Adams, Max. *The Screenwriter's Survival Guide*. New York: Warner Brothers, 2001.

Brenner, Alfred. *The TV Scriptwriter's Handbook: Dramatic Writing for Television and Film*. Los Angeles: Silman-James, 1992.

Cooper, Dona. *Writing Great Plays for Film and TV*. New York: Macmillan, 1997.

Field, Syd. *The Screenwriter's Workbook*. New York: Dell Publishing, 1984.

Flynn, Denny Martin. *How Not to Write a Screenplay: 101 Common Mistakes Most Screenwriters Make*. Los Angeles: Lone Eagle Publishing Company, 1999.

Giles, D. B. *The Screenwriter Within: How to Turn the Movie in Your Head into a Salable Screenplay*. New York: Three Rivers Press, 2000.

Hauge, Michael. *Writing Screenplays That Sell*. New York: Harperperrenial Library, 1991.

Keane, Christopher, and Julius Epstein. *How to Write a Selling Screenplay: A Step-By-Step Approach to Developing Your Story and Writing Your Screenplay by One of Today's Most Successful Screenwriters*. New York: Bantam Doubleday Dell Publishing, 1998.

Maselo, Robert. *A Friend in the Business: Honest Advice for Anyone Trying to Break into Television Writing*. New York: Perigree, 2000.

Press, Skip. *The Complete Idiot's Guide to Screenwriting*. Falls Church, VA: Alpha Books, 2001.

Resnik, Gail, and Scott Trost. *All You Need to Know About the Movie and TV Business*. New York: Fireside, 1996.

Russell, James. *Screen & Stage Marketing Secret*s. Reno, NV: James Russell Publishing, 1998.

Sautter, Carl. *How to Sell Your Screenplay*. New York: New Chapter Press, 1992.

Seger, Linda. *Making a Good Writer Great: A Creativity Workbook for Screenwriters*. Los Angeles: Silman-James Press, 1999.

Smith, Evan S. *Writing Television Sitcoms*. New York: Perigree, 1999.

Trottier, David. *The Screenwriter's Bible*. Beverly Hills, CA: Silman-James Press, 1998.

Wong, Chi-Li, and Kenneth J. Atchity. *Writing Treatments That Sell: How to Create and Market Your Story Ideas to the Motion Picture and TV Industry*. New York: Henry Holt, 1997.

SOFTWARE

Final Draft Professional Screenwriting Software (available exclusively from http://www.finaldraft.com) is available for use by both Mac and PC users and has all the formatting required for screenplays and teleplays built in.

7

PRODUCTION ASSISTANT

Production assistants, or PAs as they are commonly called, are the people who do just about the most work in the film and television industry. This is a terrific first job for someone wishing to work behind the scenes in television and film. Production assistants are perhaps the most valuable people in the industry. Although this may be considered an entry-level position in the industry, a good production assistant who enjoys his or her work may do this for years, making a good career for himself or herself. Either way, you will gain a great deal of industry experience before taking advantage of all the room for career advancement.

The PA runs around taking care of all the little details that keep things moving smoothly. Your responsibilities may range from bringing the director coffee every morning to keeping pedestrians from walking down the street during the shooting of a scene. You help everyone who needs you. You must stay on your toes at all times, anticipating the needs of those you work with most closely. As a PA you will be exposed to just about every aspect of the industry. A good PA will quickly earn respect, and not long after that, a promotion. When you are ready to advance in your career, you will have had such great experiences in so many areas it may simply be a matter of choosing which field you like best.

Earnings

The typical production assistant can expect to earn an average of $200 to $400 per week. No, it is not great pay, but the experience you gain will compensate. On the other hand, if you get in with a good company on a high-budget film, the money could be very good.

A production assistant checks the makeup of Native American extras as other extras stand by during filming of *Around the World in 80 Days.*

FOR MORE INFORMATION

ASSOCIATIONS

The Directors Guild of America—East Coast Office
110 West 57th Street, 2nd Floor
New York, NY 10019
(212) 581-0370

The Directors Guild of America—Midwest Office
400 North Michigan Avenue, Suite 307
Chicago, IL 60611
(312) 644-5050

The Directors Guild of America—West Coast Office
7920 Sunset Boulevard
Los Angeles, CA 90046
(310) 289-2000

Illinois Film Office
100 W. Randolph
Chicago, IL 60601
(312) 427-FILM (3456)

BOOKS

Alves, Jeff. *How to Break into the Film Business: The Production Assistant Handbook*. Los Angeles: Players Press, 1991.

Farle, Mark. T*he Production Assistant's Handbook*. Available exclusively from http://www.employnow.com/pa.htm.

Hart, Douglas C. *The Camera Assistant: A Complete Professional Handbook*. Boston: Focal Press, 1995.

Heath, David. *Television Production Assistant (Careers Without College)*. Minnetonka, MN: Capstone Press, 1999.

WEB SITES

Channel 4 Television — PURE
http://www.channel4.com/plus/pure/crew.html

Experience Magazine
http://www.experience.com

The Indepth Interview
http://members.aol.com/rogueisis/interview.html

Job Circle
http://www.jobcircle.com/career/articles/98.html

TRADE JOURNALS

Ross Reports Television and Film
1515 Broadway, 14th Floor
New York, NY 10036
(800) 817-3273

Variety
P.O. Box 15878
North Hollywood, CA 91615-5878
(800) 323-4345

SCRIPT SUPERVISOR

A script supervisor has a lot more work to do than simply supervising the script. Another name for a script supervisor is continuity expert or continuity supervisor. This makes a little more sense when you see what the job responsibilities really entail. As a script supervisor, you will be responsible for keeping a very detailed, written account of all the scenes filmed or taped during a production. This is very important because the scenes of television shows and movies are not shot in the sequence in which they appear in the final production. The script supervisor's job is to keep notes that will be referred to day after day to be sure that the action matches from one take or scene to another. In other words, the script supervisor is responsible for making sure that the film looks like it has been shot in sequence. Most films are shot on a schedule that must balance such factors as the availability of actors and the availability of locations, to mention just two considerations. For example, when the movie *Titanic* was being filmed, all of the scenes featuring the character Molly Brown, played by Kathy Bates, were shot within just a few days. Yet as you watch the movie, you will notice that Molly Brown appears throughout the film. It is the script supervisor's job to make sure that the hair, makeup, costumes, dialogue, and props all match from one scene to the next.

This is a job for someone with a great deal of patience, a terrific eye for detail, and a great memory. You will also need to be very well organized to do this kind of work. If you are good at taking notes, this may be a good job for

A script supervisor and his assistant go over their notes before a scene is filmed. The set must look exactly as it did during previous "takes."

you. You will have to write notes detailing just about everything that happens each time the camera rolls. You will have to record what the shot looked like and how long it took. You must note which camera was used and exactly how the actors were positioned. You have to take note of it all and make sure that the scene is set exactly the same way each time the camera rolls, even if days have passed since the last shoot. The next time you watch *The Wizard of Oz*, pay attention to the length of Dorothy's pigtails. Throughout the film they go from just about shoulder length to quite long and back again. Now, unless there was a hairstylist giving free haircuts along the Yellow Brick Road, this is a very good example of a script supervisor who was *not* keeping detailed notes!

The script supervisor works directly with the director of the film or television show to be sure that all necessary shots have been done, that there are no big mistakes in screen direction or the continuing action, and that scenes will all edit together cleanly. The camera department will check with the script supervisor to be sure that each scene is listed correctly, to make sure their logs and reports agree, and to record focal lengths and filters for matching shots later on. You will work closely with the heads of other departments to ensure that makeup, wardrobe, hair, props, set dressing, and everything else has the proper continuity. You may assist the actors by helping them with their lines, reminding them what they did or how they performed an action in a previous take, and making sure that the script matches any ad libs or mistakes the actors have made. It is important that you make your notes with great detail. Your notes will help the editor identify the shots he or she must piece together to make a complete film.

The production office will rely on you to provide them with important information each day, such as how many scenes were scheduled for that day and how many of those scheduled were actually completed. You will have to know the time shooting gets started each day, what time the lunch break occurred, and when shooting for the day ended.

The first thing you will do when you get a script is to break it down. This means dividing the scenes, discovering and noting their chronological order and the day each scene takes place, counting the total scenes and total pages, and giving a one-line synopsis of all of this information. You might be asked to time the entire script. You will also have to attend production meetings.

Every day you will be responsible for preparing each of the pages of the script that will be shot that day. In addition, you will also prepare all logs and reports, and record the time of the first shot of the day. For each shot you will have to time the rehearsals and make notes about them. You will then have to figure out what scene number the shot will be

Script supervisor Susan Malerstein-Watkins *(left)* and director Frank Darabont watch a take on the video replay monitors at the Old Tennessee State Prison in Nashville, Tennessee, during the filming of *The Green Mile*.

called, and let the camera and sound departments know. It is essential that you keep track of the scene number, camera and sound rolls, and scene description each time a scene is set up. You will write down the take number, the length of the take, how the take went, and which take or takes the director particularly liked.

Toward the middle of the day the cast and crew will break for lunch. At this point, you will note the time and a lot of other things as well. You will need to have notes on what was going on before lunch and what is to happen directly after lunch. The fact that lunch was called should not interfere with the continuity of the shooting schedule. Later, when the day is over, you will have to check in with the sound and camera people to coordinate which takes the director likes and might use in the final cut. You will have notes on everything that happened that day and you will hand in copies of those notes to the production department. It may be up to you to determine what time shooting should begin the next day. You are the one responsible for making sure that all the little details of the filming go smoothly.

Training

Script supervising is another career that is basically learned on the job. You may find a workshop or two out there, like the one suggested in the following directory under Web sites. Basically, however, you just need to possess a certain set of skills. These are organization, discipline, attention to detail, observation, good memory, and good handwriting. You will do well to have some background knowledge in the workings of film and television. This will mostly come from experience, but you should at least have an idea of what is going on and what things are called.

Script supervisors do not have assistants to help them out. You are the one person responsible for everything listed earlier. Many people in the cast and crew rely heavily on you. Be there. Be on time. Do your job with perfection. You may start out working for little or no money on low budget films or commercials. Use these paths to gain experience so that when you are asked to work on a major motion picture or a television show, you are already an old pro at what you do!

FOR MORE INFORMATION

WEB SITES

Film and TV Connection
http://www.film-connection.com/

Film Continuity & Script Supervising Workshop
http://www.theworkshops.com/filmworkshops

BOOKS

Buzzell, Linda. *How to Make It in Hollywood: All the Right Moves*. New York: Harperperrenial, 1996.

Fitzsimmons, April. *Breaking & Entering: Land Your First Job in Film Production*. Los Angeles: Lone Eagle, 1997.

Levy, Frederick. *Hollywood 101: The Film Industry*. Los Angeles: Renaissance Books, 2000.

Miller, Pat P. *Script Supervising and Film Continuity*. Oxford, England: Focal Press (Butterworth-Heinemann), 1999.

Resnik, Gail, and Scott Trost. *All You Need to Know About the Movie and TV Business*. New York: Fireside, 1996.

Rowlands, Avril. *Continuity in Film and Video*. Boston: Focal Press Media Manuals Series, 1989.

Taylor, Hugh. *The Hollywood Job-Hunter's Survival Guide: An Insider's Winning Strategies for Getting That All-Important First Job and Keeping It*. Los Angeles: Lone Eagle, 1992.

Ulmer, Shirley, and C. R. Sevilla. *The Role of the Script Supervisor in Film and Television*. Emeryville, CA: Hastings House, 1987.

TRADE JOURNALS

MovieMaker
2265 Westwood Blvd. #479
Los Angeles, CA 90064
(310) 234-9234
Web site: http://www.moviemaker.com

9

LOCATION SCOUT

Before considering a career as a location scout, you must first understand what is meant by "location." Location, in this business, basically means outside of a studio. Most films are shot on location, whereas most weekly television shows are not. If you have a good eye and like to travel around, you may be interested in finding work as a location scout.

A location scout does exactly what the job title indicates. He or she travels around scouting, or looking for, locations to shoot scenes for a film. This is good work for a person who has a good memory and a good eye and likes to travel. First, you will read the film's script. Then you will have a discussion with the location manager to figure out exactly what it is you will be looking for in a location. Then off you go with your camera to find the perfect setting to shoot the film. A location scout works closely with the location manager to help find locations in which to film a movie.

The location scout has quite a bit of responsibility. As the location manager's right-hand person, he or she assists the location manager in getting appropriate, photogenic locations for filming. He or she helps negotiate the price of shooting at that location. He or she keeps a written record of all the details of the locations needed and when they must be secured. He or she travels to the location and gathers all relevant information, such as the location's exact address, the phone number, contact person, usage fee, and availability of the location. Then he or she takes photographs of the location and notes the time of day and the direction the camera is pointed so that the director can see how things will look as he or she shoots film at various times of the day or night. The location scout must be very careful with details. He or she must note many important features of the location, such as

A location scout videotapes a spot in New York City that she will recommend to the location manager.

existing power sources and the ease of transporting film equipment to that location. The location scout checks the availability and convenience of parking, as well as whether or not there are restaurants or places nearby for the crew to get food. The location scout finds out if permits or special rules restrict usage of the area. He or she also must write down the condition of the location and decide whether or not any special work must be done before filming starts. The location scout checks things like noises from nearby activities, lighting conditions, road conditions, and so on.

As a location scout, it is not only your responsibility to find the perfect spot to shoot the film; it is also your responsibility to get the necessary permission to shoot at that spot. This may involve asking a homeowner if the film crew can shoot on his or her property. Or it may become a much bigger deal if the location is a place of high security or a busy venue that requires some juggling to get a film crew in and around everyday people. Shooting in a big city can create such headaches, but many cities have agencies that assist location scouts to encourage the making of movies or television shows in their municipality.

The location scout has his or her own bag of tools to get the job done. To do this work well, you will need maps, a tape measure, a 35mm camera, a Polaroid or digital camera, a video camera, a compass, tape, pens, paper, folders, company business cards, a cell phone, a beeper, transportation, and a good memory. You will also need a working knowledge of basic architecture. You must be able to describe accurately the buildings at a particular location and to recognize that their style of construction fits the period of the film. Organizational skills are important to a career of this type, too, because the location scout must put together all this information in a folder that is given to the location manager.

The production team for the film *American Leather* has photographs of potential shooting locations on the wall of their office.

As you advance in your career, your first step up will be to the position of location manager. The location manager is responsible for weeding out the locations that cannot be used and then presenting the possible options to the film's director. Not only does he or she have to decide whether the potential location fits the needs of the script; he or she also has to figure out whether the potential location is accessible to the cast and crew with all of their equipment.

The location manager then becomes a negotiator. If the potential location happens to be a home occupied by a family, that home will have to be rented by the film crew. The location manager negotiates the rental price as well as plans to repair any damage that may occur during filming. The film crew generally prefers that the family stay elsewhere during the shooting, and that, too, must be negotiated. Once these tasks are accomplished, the location manager gets busy obtaining the proper permits and insurance to film on the chosen location. On the day of filming, he or she makes sure that everything is as it should be and then he or she is off until the end of the shoot, when he returns to be sure everything is still as it should be.

This is a freelance job, which means that you work for yourself, getting jobs where you can. You will get paid for each job you do. If a production company likes your work, you may find yourself steadily employed by that company. As you build your location managing skills, you may soon be ready to advance to a more prestigious career. You may soon find yourself following the career path of film producer!

The location manager is one of the very first people to be hired to work on a project. Location managers must be extremely diplomatic, as they are responsible for maintaining a good relationship between the movie company and the community in which they are filming.

FOR MORE INFORMATION

ASSOCIATIONS

Association of Film Commissioners International
Administrative Office
P.O. Box 1419
314 N. Main Street, 3rd Floor
Helena, MT 59624
(406)495-8045
e-mail: afci@afci.org
Web site: http://www.afci.org

Location Association
(323) 656-3999
Web site: http://www.locationassociation.com
"Feel free to e-mail us at locationa@aol.com with your questions. You can also contact Dave Denny at our Los Angeles, CA, office."

Locations **Magazine**
Association of Film Commissioners International
c/o Wyoming Film Office
I-25 & College Drive
Cheyenne, WY 82002
(307) 637-3601

Locations Scouting and Management
Web site: http://home.earthlink.net/~ronabrams/

WEB SITES

@LA
http://www.at-la.com/@la-film/sets.htm#loc

Location Scout 360 at Lions Gate Studios
http://www.locationscout360.com

Locations Scouting and Management
http://home.earthlink.net/~ronabrams/

www.Locationscout.com
http://www.locationscout.com/

BOOKS

Maier, Robert G. *Location Scouting and Management Handbook: Television, Film, Still Photography*. Boston: Focal Press, 1994.

Shonfield, Katherine. *Walls Have Feelings: Architecture, Film and the City*. New York: Routledge, 2000.

TRADE JOURNALS

Birns & Sawyer, Inc. Catalog
1026 N. Highland Ave.
Hollywood, CA 90038
(323) 466-8211

THE GRIP

A grip is a person who moves this and that from here to there and helps to set up things on the set. There are several types of grips: the key grip, the dolly grip, and the best boy grip. None have anything to do with keys or dolls, and the best boy can be female. Grips are strong people in good physical condition. They know all of the equipment

88

on the set and understand how it is used. If you go this route, you will be moving things around the set. Therefore, you have to know what everything is and how it works. You may help out with the camera and lights as well as with props.

The head of the grips is the key grip. He or she is responsible for hiring a good team of workers to get the film made, and is also in charge of renting the equipment the crew will need for the shoot. Each city has its own equipment rental house. As a key grip, you may eventually accumulate your own equipment, which will mean that the production company will have to pay you for the use of this equipment. You will be required to read the script of the production you are working on and set up the necessary equipment to shoot each scene. You will also need to know what lights are needed. The only way to know these things is through experience. To get experience you must start at the bottom of the grip pile and work your way up. You may even have to start as a volunteer on a production.

Let us take a look at the ranking of grips by going down the ladder. The top position, as noted earlier, is the key grip. The key grip's assistant is called the best boy grip. The best boy is officially known as the assistant key grip or the assistant chief lighting technician. He or she is second in command to the key grip. Before you get there you will probably work as a dolly grip after you have mastered some of

Grips help the cameraman move the dolly back and forth on a track during the shooting of *Robocop*.

the basics during your time as a hard-working volunteer. A dolly is a camera on wheels that can be manually positioned to get the shot just right. The dolly grip is the person who moves this camera mounting back and forth to get the shot. You need to be strong and have smooth movement so that the dolly moves without bumping or jerking. Sometimes you will also have to raise and lower a crane arm to get the camera in the right position. All of this comes after you have mastered your understanding of the machinery you are using.

FOR MORE INFORMATION

ASSOCIATIONS

IATSE (International Alliance of Theatrical Stage Employees)
http://www.iatse.lm.com/index.html

WEB SITES

@LA
http://www.at-la.com/@la-film/equip.htm#light

BOOKS

Taub, Eric. *Gaffers, Grips, and Best Boys*. New York: St. Martin's Press, 1995.

Uva, Michael, and Sabrina Uva. *The Grip Book*. Pico Rivera, CA: Kater-Crafts. Inc., 1997.

11

THE GAFFER

As head electrician or chief lighting technician, the gaffer is the head of the electrical department, responsible for overseeing all things electric on the set. He or she is responsible for designing and executing the lighting plan for a film or television production. He or she and the crew of electricians provide, set up, and strike

(take down) all the lights. He or she also coordinates with the director of photography to develop the particular look required for a scene or effect.

You will need a background as an electrician to do this kind of work. As gaffer, your main job is to make the scene look the way the director and the director of photography envision it. You will have to know how lights work and what they can and cannot do. You will need to understand the different lighting requirements needed to make a room eerie, cheerful, calm, or tense. You will need to have a very good understanding of the film stock or video equipment that is being used, as well as the lighting equipment and techniques. You also must be good at taking charge and delegating responsibility. You are also responsible for accurately estimating the time it will take to do each setup so that the actors and others working on the project can be scheduled to come in at the right time.

The gaffer will light the scene and let the actors walk through it. You must be very observant, noting the shadows and what works and what does not. Then you make the necessary changes for the scene, and the scene is ready to be shot.

Training

The best training for lighting work, as with most of the work in this industry, is experience. Work with the lighting crew of

Crew members adjust lights on a movie set.

as many high school theatrical productions as you can. Then move on to community theater. What you learn working in the theater will be your most valuable training. You will find that lighting is a complex and highly skilled craft that sets the tone of a film as much as set design or camera angle. Professional gaffers are true artists.

FOR MORE INFORMATION

ASSOCIATIONS

IATSE (International Alliance of Theatrical Stage Employees)
http://www.iatse.lm.com/index.html

BOOKS

Box, Harry. *The Set Technician's Lighting Handbook*. Boston: Focal Press, 1997.

Fitt, Brian. *The Gaffer's Handbook: Film Lighting Equipment, Practice, and Electrical Distributio*n. London: William Heinemann, 1998.

Malkiewicz, Kris, Leonard Konopelski, and Barbara J. Gryboski. *Film Lighting: Talks with Hollywood's Cinematographers and Gaffers*. New York: Simon & Schuster, 1992.

Taub, Eric. *Gaffers, Grips, and Best Boys*. New York: St. Martin's Press, 1995.

WEB SITES

Backstage Jobs
http://backstagejobs.com/

Cely Communications, Inc.
http://www.cely.com/lighting/gaffer.html

12

WARDROBE

One of the most creative behind-the-scenes film careers is the one in which you get to make the actors look like the characters they are playing. The costumes used in a television show or a film may simply be everyday clothes, which perhaps only need a bit of tailoring. But they could be elaborate futuristic garments, such as you would see on a television show like *Star Trek*, or period costumes, as in the movie *Titanic*. Wardrobe people are responsible for making, arranging, and taking care of all of the costumes and accessories that are worn by actors and extras in a television or film production. Other titles you may hear are wardrobe assistant, wardrobe master/mistress, costume designer, costume supervisor, costumer, wardrobe coordinator, or key costumer. Each of these jobs is slightly different, depending on the level of experience and responsibility. Let us just talk about working in the wardrobe department in general.

The wardrobe people do many things. First they must have a discussion with the production designer and the director to decide what type of costumes and accessories are going to be used in the production. Next the wardrobe person must design and then either find or make all of the costumes and accessories that will be worn. To do this, he or she often has to do some research to find out what clothes from a particular period looked like. The wardrobe person works very closely with the director and the script supervisor to make sure that the costumes look as they are supposed to from one scene to the next.

The wardrobe person also needs to be sure that each costume looks right under the lights that will be used in filming. Sometimes the costumers spend a great deal of time searching retail stores and resale shops for appropriate costume

A wardrobe assistant discusses the design and fabric for a costume with director Federico Fellini during the making of *The Clowns* in 1971.

pieces. For other projects, the costume crew may actually be responsible for creating the costumes from scratch.

The costume designer is the main talent behind the costumes. As with most behind-the-scenes work, as a costume designer you will first have to read the script for the television show or the film. You will sketch out your costume ideas as they come to mind. Then it will be your responsibility to produce these costumes and be sure they fit the actors properly. You work on the set the first day each costume is used during the shoot to be sure that it really looks the way it is expected to look. You will be responsible for fixing anything that may go wrong, like a split seem or a broken zipper. Your costume supervisor will be there to help you with these tasks. He or she will also keep all the paperwork on the costumes. Your key costumer will maintain the integrity of the costumes from day to day. Just as the script supervisor oversees the continuity from one shot to another, the key costumer takes great pains to ensure that the costumes look the same on the last day of shooting as they did on the first day. The key costumer is also the one who works the closest with the actors. You get to tell the actors which costumes to wear, when to wear them, and how to wear them. People on the wardrobe team are responsible for such tasks as making and cutting out patterns, altering costumes to fit the actors, cleaning and repairing the costumes, and dressing actors.

The wardrobe person must have a good understanding of many of the properties of fabrics, such as how durable they are, how well they dye, which types work best under certain lights, and other such matters. He or she must also have a background in costume, fashion, and fabric history. A particular fabric might look terrific on an actor playing a certain role, but if it's a period piece, it's going to be important to know whether or not that type of fabric was worn, or even if it existed at that time in history. Of course you will also need an eye for the basics: color, texture, and shape. In addition to pos-

A costumer works on the sleeve of a Victorian-style dress.

sessing obvious talents such as good measuring, pattern-making, cutting, and sewing skills, an eye for detail, and strong design and planning skills, a wardrobe person should also have solid contract negotiating skills, computer skills, and a lot of self-motivation.

Training

If you have been sewing for years, most likely you will not need any extensive training. Let us assume that you are a

real sewing buff and that is why you are considering choosing this career path. The more experience you can put on your résumé, the better. Wardrobe people generally gain their skills on the job. However, to give yourself an advantage, you should take classes in fashion, clothing, design, and textiles. Consider also taking classes in film, drama, and theater. Your high school may offer some of these courses. Check with your local community college or your local sewing or fabric store for these classes. The more experience you can bring to your career as you begin, the better. Volunteer to help with costumes, or even to oversee costumes, for community theaters and university or community college theater departments in your area. Consider working after school for a local dress shop, a bridal shop, or a tailor.

Pay

Although pay for wardrobe people varies, it is safe to say that you will earn an average of $10 to $20 per hour. You may be paid in one lump sum for a production. At the top of the profession, if you are the costume designer or wardrobe master/mistress, you could earn as much as $2,300 per week. As wardrobe people are often self-employed, they find work from film to film, often on short-term contracts. Expect to work long, sometimes irregular hours, sometimes for days at a time, and even on weekends or evenings to get a project done.

FOR MORE INFORMATION

WEB SITES

Kiwi Careers
http://www.careers.co.nz

Manhattan Wardrobe Supply
http://www.wardrobesupplies.com

Wardrobe Solutions
http://www.indienews.com

BOOKS

Gorsline, Douglas W. *What People Wore: 1,800 Illustrations from Ancient Times to the Early Twentieth Century*. Mineola: Dover Publishers, 1994.

Kid, Mary T. *Stage Costume Step-By-Step: The Complete Guide to Designing and Making Stage Costumes for All Major Drama Periods and Genres from Classical Through the Twentieth Century*. Cincinnati, OH: Betterway Books, 1996.

Panicelli, Ida. *Fellini: Costumes and Fashion*. Milan, Italy: Charta, 1996.

THE MAKEUP ARTIST

The makeup artist is the first person the actor works with when he or she arrives on the set each day. Makeup is worn by all actors. The makeup artist may simply cover some blemishes and bring out an actor's features. He or she may help a young person look as if he or she has aged several years. The makeup artist may transform a man

A makeup artist prepares an actor for a scene.

to look like a woman, like some of Eddie Murphy's characters in the film *Nutty Professor II*. Or, as in the film *How the Grinch Stole Christmas*, the makeup artist may completely transform an actor's features into a particular character.

Obviously, then, to be a makeup artist you really need to like to do makeup. You need to be artistic, and you must be very good with details. Once again, what the actor looks like in one shot on one day is exactly how he or she needs to appear in the next shot on another day. It will be up to you to apply each actor's makeup in exactly the same way from

Eddie Murphy, dressed as a woman, in a scene from the movie *The Nutty Professor*

day to day. You will work closely not only with the director and the costumer but also with the hairdresser.

Training

Although you certainly need artistic talent more than you need a college education for a career in makeup, you will have to take a few classes and read plenty of books and practice, practice, practice if you want a career in this field. Work in the theater department of your high school and do some community theater. Work with as many theatrical productions as you can. The more different types of makeup you have to do, the more you will learn. Work on shows that require you to learn old-age makeup, animal faces, and special effects.

It is important to note, however, that there is a big difference between the makeup techniques used for the stage and makeup used for film. It will be necessary for you to not only know the difference, but know how to do both kinds of makeup.

FOR MORE INFORMATION

CLASSES

Elegance International
Hollywood, CA
(323) 937-4838
e-mail: TwoFacesMakeup@aol.com

The Institute of Studio Makeup, Ltd.
3497 Cahuenga Boulevard West
Hollywood, CA 90068-1338
(213) 850-6661

WEB SITES

Makeup Artist Network
http://www.makeupart.net

BOOKS

Buchman, Herman. *Stage Makeup*. New York: Watson-Guptil Publications, 1989.

Corson, Richard. *Stage Makeup*. Englewood Cliffs, NJ: Prentice Hall, 1985.

Frank, Vivien, and Deborah Jaffe. *Making Masks*. Syracuse, NY: Chartwell Books, 1992.

Kehoe, Vincent J. R. *Special Make-Up Effects*. Boston: Focal Press, 1991.

Place, Stan Campbell. *The Art and Science of Professional Makeup*. Tarrytown: Milday Publishing Co., 1990.

Swinfield, Rosemarie. *Stage Makeup*. Cincinnati, OH: Betterway Books, 2000.

MAKEUP ARTISTS

Andrea Nichols, Inc.
6270 N. Leona
Chicago, IL 60646
(312) 851-6754

Jeffrey Segal Studio
1040 W. Huron
Chicago, IL 60622
(312) 563-9368

SPECIAL EFFECTS ARTIST

There are quite a few sub-specialties that can be listed under the general heading of special effects artist. Basically, however, a special effects artist is someone who makes things happen in the movies or on television that would not normally occur in real life.

Special effects have been showing up in the movies for 100

years. But it wasn't until 1977, when the movie *Star Wars* broke new ground with special effects, that the actual field of special effects became one of the most popular and fastest growing in the film industry. Within the broad field of special effects arts are career possibilities in computer effects, creature effects, visual effects, and puppetry.

The computer effects artist must have a background in animation and a general technical background in computers in order to do computer graphic images. Computer graphic or digital images are often used when filming the real thing might be too difficult, dangerous, or expensive. For example, a scene may call for six dolphins to jump simultaneously, creating a beautiful arc over a sunset. Trying to get this shot from nature might be next to impossible. That's where computer graphics come in. The computer effects artist works on his or her computer to create the image, making it look so real that filmgoers will have no idea that they are not watching an authentic nature shot.

The creature effects artist creates unique creatures that no one has seen before. He or she uses imagination and talent to think up and create creatures that fit the director's needs as dictated by the script. The creature designer must first read the script and see what is needed for the story. Then, using previous art training, he or she will create what is necessary for the film. With help from a sculptor, mold maker, foam latex runner, painter, and mechanic, the

A scene from *The Matrix* in which two characters, played by Keanu Reeves *(left)* and Hugo Weaving, experience suspended motion.

creature effects artist produces an exciting new creature for each film.

If your background leans more toward mechanics, you might look toward a career as a creature effects mechanic. This is the person who creates the framework and musculature of the creature so that it can move and function properly. He or she is responsible for putting in the controls to move the creature's face and limbs. The mechanic is the tinkerer, the person who is always curious to know how all of the little gadgets and doodads work. He or she needs to

A computer animation specialist uses a wand to trace the shape of a model spacecraft directly into a computer's memory, allowing the machine to "know" the exact dimensions of the plane.

understand mechanical parts and how they can be put together to work. An understanding of air compressors and hydraulics as used for movement is a must. An understanding of electronics will also help you.

Training

The special effects artist needs a background in the arts, which includes drawing, sculpting, and fine arts. Take as many art classes as you can. A mechanical background is of great help as well. Take classes that deal with mechanical things, like shop. Special effects artists often have specialized knowledge that can only be obtained in specific ways, such as learning to handle explosives, which may require a military background.

FOR MORE INFORMATION

CLASSES

The Institute of Studio Makeup, Ltd.
3497 Cahuenga Boulevard West
Hollywood, CA 90068-1338
(213) 850-6661

BOOKS

Blair, Preston. *Cartoon Animation*. Laguna Hills, CA: Walter Foster Publishers, 1995.

Cosner, Shaaron. *Special Effects in Movies and TV*. New York: J. Messner, 1985.

Fielding, Raymond. *The Technique of Special Effects Cinematography*. Boston: Focal Press, 1985.

Goulekas, Karen E. *Visual Effects in a Digital World: A Comprehensive Glossary of Over 7,000 Visual Effects Terms*. San Francisco, CA: Morgan Kaufmann Publishers, 2001.

Hamilton, Jake. *Special Effects in Film and Television*. New York: DK Publishing, 1998.

Hutchison, David. *Film Magic: The Art and Science of Special Effects*. New York: Prentice-Hall, 1987.

Kehoe, Vincent J. R. *Special Make-Up Effects*. Boston: Focal Press, 1991.

McKenzie, Alan, and Derek Ware. *Hollywood Tricks of the Trade*. New York: Gallery Books, 1986.

Powers, Tom. *Special Effects in the Movies*. San Diego, CA: Lucent Books, 1989.

Rickitt, Richard. *Special Effects*. New York: Watson-Guptill, 2000.

Rogers, Pauline B. *The Art of Visual Effects: Interviews on the Tools of the Trade*. Boston: Focal Press, 1999.

Schecter, Harold, and David Everitt. *Film Tricks: Special Effects in the Movies*. New York: Harlan Quist, 1981.

Timpone, Anthony. *Men, Makeup, and Monsters: Hollywood's Masters of Illusion and FX*. New York: St. Martin's Griffin, 1996.

Wilkie, Bernard. *Creating Special Effects for TV and Video*. Boston: Focal Press, 1991.

MAGAZINES

Cinefex
P.O. Box 20027
Riverside, CA 92516
(714) 242-9704

Computer Graphics World
Web site: http://cgw.pennnet.com

15

ANIMATOR

An animator is someone who turns drawings and inanimate objects into moving, believable characters. There are several types of animation. Stop motion animation, claymation, and digital effects animation are a few of the different fields you might find yourself working in.

Stop motion animators animate creatures for films and television shows by photographing small changes in the position of models. Because stop motion animation is a time-consuming process, it requires a significant amount of patience. A stop motion artist animates a creature by posing it for each single frame of film. For each frame, the stop motion animator must move the creature just a tiny bit so that the motion looks smooth and fluid and as natural as possible when the film rolls. There are twenty-four frames in one second of film. This means that a stop motion animator might move a creature several thousand times for just a few minutes of film.

A claymation animator does pretty much the same job as the stop motion animator, except that he or she works with clay characters that must be resculpted to show their movements from frame to frame. The digital effects animator manipulates computer images and can create effects that look spectacular on film.

Training

Animators need a strong background in art and cinematography. Computer skills are important, too. Fortunately, animation is something that you can experiment with on your own. A modest investment in equipment will enable you to learn how to make characters move properly and make your own animated films.

A scene from the claymation movie *Chicken Run*. In claymation, the animator photographs a clay model with a wire frame.

FOR MORE INFORMATION

FILM SCHOOLS

The American Film Institute
2021 North Western Avenue
Los Angeles, CA 90027
(323) 856-7600

The American Film Institute
The John F. Kennedy Center for the Performing Arts
Washington, DC 20566
(202) 833-AFIT (2348)

Motion Picture Pro Studios
122 West 26th Street, Suite 1001
New York NY 10001
(212) 691-7791

WEB SITES

Animation World Network
http://www.awn.com

BOOKS

Culhane, Shamus. *Animation from Script to Screen*. New York: St. Martin's Press, 1990.

Fielding, Raymond. *Techniques of Special Effects Cinematography*. Stoneham, MA: Focal Press, 1985.

Gray, Milton. *Cartoon Animation: Introduction to a Career*. Northridge, CA: Lion's Den Productions, 1991.

Halas, John. *The Contemporary Animator*. Oxford: Butterworth-Heinemann, 1990.

Layboume, Kit. *The Animation Book: A Complete Guide to Animated Filmmaking From Flip-Books to Sound Cartoons*. New York: Three Rivers Press, 1998.

Pintoff, Ernest. *The Complete Guide to American Film Schools and Cinema and Television Courses*. New York: Penguin USA, 1994.

Pintoff, Ernest. *The Complete Guide to Animation and Computer Graphics Schools*. New York: Watson-Guptill, 1995.

16

FOLEY ARTIST

A Foley artist is the person who creates sound effects for film and television shows. Often the sounds that you hear when you are watching a movie were put in later, after the filming was complete. This is because it would be quite distracting to have all of the sounds going off at once, as in real life. The actors might become rattled and miss their lines. The Foley artist mixes the sounds so that they balance well and the audience can appreciate them. The Foley artist produces that sound in a studio called the Foley stage. A Foley stage is really just a very large soundproof room that is designed for the re-creation of real-life sounds. The Foley artist watches the edited version of the film. While doing so, he or she must match the sound effects exactly to the movements in the film. The idea is to put realism into the film.

In the soundproof studio you will also find Foley pits. These are actual pits or containers for different kinds of debris—water, dirt, mud, gravel, sand, and rock. Foley artists specialize in recreating the sounds of footsteps, people running, walking, crawling, and splashing in sync with the action on the screen. He or she creates these sounds by using different types of shoes on different surface materials. The Foley artist also uses an amazing variety of props, such as car fenders, chairs, glasses, plates, and just about anything else that can be found, to make unusual sounds.

The Foley artist is an expert at creating sounds that mimic those of real life. This is necessary because on the

A Foley artist presses keys on his control board to create and blend sounds into a movie.

set of a film almost nothing is real. The Foley artist also puts in all the background noises that make the scene seem more real. When the film is edited together for a final product, it is very important that the sound flows neatly from one moment to the next. The Foley artist has the important job of making sure that the film sounds as good as it looks.

Training

This is another one of those careers in which experience proves to be your best training. Check out your local radio station to see if the DJs use sound effects. An internship there would be a good place to start. Of course, you can also start by making sounds in your own home. Record what you do and ask people to identify the sounds. If they can tell what the sounds are, you are doing a good job. Work in your high school theater department or in the local community theater and do all of the sounds needed for the shows. You can find tapes of sound effects at your local library. Use them to practice and perfect your craft. A good Foley artist may earn up to $400 a day.

The Future

The future of the Foley artist is in digital sound effects. This means that instead of using real objects to make sounds, Foley artists will simply be pressing the keys on a synthesizer

control board. As a result, computer skills will become more valuable to Foley artists in the future.

FOR MORE INFORMATION

WEB SITES

Warner Bros. Studios Facilities Post Production Services
http://wbsf.wanerbros.com

Find out about internships by contacting Warner Bros. at
Warner Bros. Studios
4000 Warner Boulevard, Building 4
Burbank, CA 91522
(818) 954-2515

or

Warner Bros. Studios
1041 North Formosa Avenue
West Hollywood, CA 90046
(323) 850-2581
Wavegroup Sound
http://www.wavegroup.com
(408) 727-8444

BOOKS

Holman, Tomlinson. *Sound for Film and Television*. Boston: Focal Press, 1997.

Lobrutto, Vincent. *Sound-on-Film*. Westport, CT: Praeger, 1994.

Tone, Kevin. *Digital Audio Post for Films on a Budget*. Seattle, WA: Sound Rangers, 1999.

Weiss, Elisabeth, and John Belton, eds. *Film Sound*. New York: Columbia University Press, 1985.

Yewdall, David L. *The Practical Art of Motion Picture Sound*. Oxford, England: Focal Press, 1999.

17

PUPPETEER

Although part of the general category of special effects, puppetry is such a specialized area that it deserves a separate discussion. Puppets are a very old art form, but Jim Henson's Muppets put a new face on puppets and puppetry, giving them an extraordinary life of their own. You may think of a puppet as simply a hand stuck into a sock with

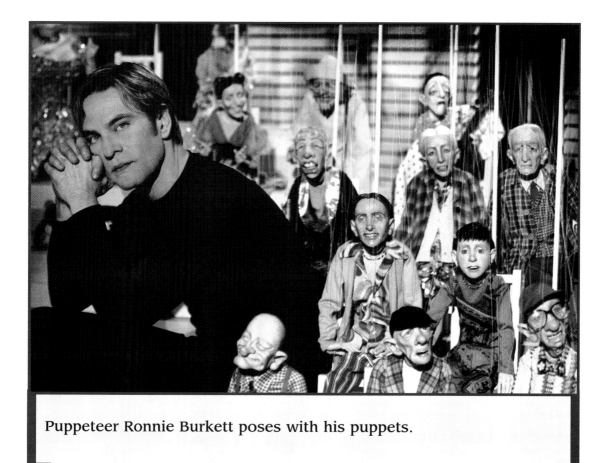

Puppeteer Ronnie Burkett poses with his puppets.

an immobile face. Not these days. Television shows such as *Sesame Street* and *Alf* and movies such as *The Empire Strikes Back (Star Wars, Episode V)* have given puppets their own identities beyond their film and television roles, and they have given puppeteers a great career path. From puppet builder all the way up to puppet supervisor, if you are willing to be silly and crazy and really take your creativity over the top, a career in puppetry may be just for you.

The arm puppets that one most commonly thinks of when one hears the word "puppet" may require several different

The actions of the Russian, a character from the Warner Bros. film *Cats & Dogs,* are a combination of puppetry, live action, and computer animation.

puppeteers to get the job done. One puppeteer may operate the actual puppet, while another operates the arms, and yet another operates the facial features, such as eyebrows, eyes, and even ears, to give the puppet lifelike expressions.

A suit performer is a puppeteer who uses his or her entire body to animate a puppet. A good example of a suit performer is the actor who works inside the big purple dinosaur costume on the children's television show *Barney.* This puppeteer is then an actor as well as a puppeteer. He must use his body in order to interpret the script.

Training

To be a suit performer you need movement training. This can be in the form of movement classes designed specifically for actors. It can also come in the form of dance training. Often the puppeteer will be responsible for providing the puppet with a voice. Voice training will help you develop a variety of different voices that you can use to give each of your different puppets a distinct personality of its own. Henson Productions holds puppeteering workshops and auditions throughout the year.

FOR MORE INFORMATION

ASSOCIATIONS

Henson Productions
117 E. 69th Street
New York, NY 10021
(212) 794-2400

Involvement Puppetry Guild of Greater New York
Box 244
New York, NY 10116
(212) 929-1568

WEB SITES

The Puppetry Home Page
http://www.sagecraft.com/puppetry

Puppets Unlimited
http://www.puppetsunlimited.com

UNICEF: Puppets with a Purpose
http://www.unicef.org/puppets

The World of Puppets
http://itdc.sbcss.k12.ca.us/curriculum/puppetry.html

PUPPET AGENTS

Communications Corporation of America
2501 N. Sheffield
Chicago, IL 60614
(773) 239-5323

PUPPETEERS

Coleman Puppet Theatre
1516 S. 2nd Avenue
Maywood, IL 60153
(708) 334-2920

Price Puppets
2430 Prairie
Evanston, IL 60201
(847) 869-6378

Puppet Parlor
1922 W. Montrose
Chicago, IL 60613
(773) 989-0308

SCHOOLS

Center for Puppetry Arts
1404 Spring Street at 18th
Atlanta, GA 30309
(404) 873-3089

National Marionette Company, Inc.
5907 N. Elston
Chicago, IL 60646
(773) 774-2919

BOOKS

Bacon, Matt. *No Strings Attached: The Inside Story of Jim Henson's Creature Shop*. New York: MacMillan, 1997.

Baird, Bil. *The Art of the Puppet*. New York: The Macmillan Company. 1965.

Beresford, Margaret. *How to Make Puppets and Teach Puppetry*. London: Mills & Boon Limited, 1966.

Binyon, Helen. *Puppetry Today*. New York: Watson-Guptil Publications, Inc., 1966.

Crothers, J. Frances. *Puppeteer's Library Guide: A Bibliographic Index to the Literature of the World Puppet Theatre*. Blue Ridge Summitt, PA: Scarecrow Press, 1971.

Lade, Roger. *The Most Excellent Book of How to Be a Puppeteer*. Brookfield, CT: Copper Beech Books, 1996.

Pettigrew, Neil. *The Stop Motion Filmography: A Critical Guide to over 325 Features Using Puppet Animation*. Jefferson, NC: McFarland and Company, 1998.

TRADE JOURNALS

Playboard
Editor, Fred Thompson
26 Howard Avenue
New Haven, CT 06519

The Puppetry Journal **(quarterly)**
Editor, Paul Eide
4923 37th Avenue S
Minneapolis, MN 55417

Puppetry Journal **(Puppeteers of America)**
4923 37th Avenue S
Minneapolis, MN 55417
(888) 568-6235

18

OTHER CAREERS

As noted previously, it is impossible in a book of this size to cover every possible career choice in the film and television industry. Movies and television shows are as diverse as life itself. An almost infinite variety of specialized skills may be called upon to make these productions more lifelike.

Therefore, if you have not found exactly what you are looking for here in terms of a career, you may want to conduct
some research of your own on some of the following career
possibilities:

- Animal trainer
- Camera operator
- Career consultant
- Carpenter
- Caterer
- Dance coordinator
- Diet consultant
- Fight coordinator
- Film director
- Film editor
- Film producer
- Painter
- Personal trainer
- Photographer
- Stand-in
- Transportation coordinator

The production designer *(left)* must use various materials and techniques to create the illusion of a particular setting for the audience. One of the important techniques at his disposal is carpentry *(above)*.

In the past, people just seemed to fall into these careers as a result of simply being in the right place at the right time when someone needed something done. To a certain extent this is still true of the film industry, but increasingly the nature of these specialized skills is being carefully defined and there are schools and apprentice programs that teach them. The point is that there are plenty of things that you can do to make a great career for yourself. Try a few different options and see what you like the best. Then work as hard as you can. You have a bright future in a fabulous career ahead of you. As they say in show business . . . break a leg!

Making it in film or television or any of the performing arts or their technical support professions means taking greater risks than a person might consider for a more conventional career. So much depends on being in the right place at the right time, and many earnest, hardworking people miss their chance. But for the successful, the reward can be fame, fortune, and a fascinating career.

GLOSSARY

AFTRA American Federation of Television and Radio Artists, one of two unions that protect actors' rights.

age range The ages that an actor can convincingly portray.

audition Tryout process used by directors to find the best person to play a role.

best boy Key grip's assistant, officially known as the assistant key grip or the assistant chief lighting technician.

dolly grip Person who moves the manual camera vehicle back and forth to get the shot.

extra Someone who works in a film or on television as part of the crowd, providing a sense of reality.

gaffer Head electrician.

grip Person who moves this and that from here to there and helps set up things on the set.

head shot An 8" x 10" black-and-white photo of yourself taken by a professional photographer.

key grip Head of the grips.

location Place outside of the studio where film is shot.

multi-listing Registering with multiple talent agents in hope of getting work.

proofs/proofsheet An 8" x 10" sheet of the thirty-six photos taken at a photo shoot from which a head shot is chosen.

résumé A written list of your credits.

SAG Screen Actors Guild, one of two unions that protect actors' rights.

slate yourself Stating your name and the role that you are auditioning for.

three-quarter shot Headshot that shows approximately three quarters of the actor, not just the actor's face.

INDEX

A

acting classes, 12–14, 23, 40–41

Act One Reports (trade magazine), 21, 33

actors, 11–27

    agents, 19–20, 28–35

    associations, 21

    directory, 23–27

    getting started, 12

    networking, 21–22

    photography, 14–17

    résumés, 17–19

    salaries, 22

    training, 12–14

AFTRA (American Federation of Television and Radio Artists), 21, 31

agents, talent, 19–20, 28–35, 39
Alf (series), 126
American Federation of
      Television and Radio Artists
      (AFTRA), 21, 31
animation, 37, 109, 114–118
animators, 114–118
  directory, 117–118
  training, 115
assistants, production, 66–70

B

Barney (series), 127
Bates, Kathy, 72
best boy grip, 88, 89
Billboard (trade magazine), 15

C

careers, other, 132–136
carpentry, 135
Chicago, 10, 19, 21, 31
claymation, 114–115, 116
computer effects, 109
continuity experts, 71
continuity supervisors, 71
costume designers, 97, 98–99
creature effects, 109–111
Cruise, Tom, 47

D

digital effects animation, 114
digital sound effects, 122–123
dolly grip, 88, 89–90

E

electricians, 92
Empire Strikes Back, The (film), 126
ER (series), 22
extras, 52–57
  directory, 55–57

F

Foley artists, 119–124
  directory, 123–124
  future of, 122–123
  training, 122
Foley stage, 120
Friends (series), 17, 22

G

gaffers, 92–95
  directory, 95
  training, 93–94
grips, 88–91
  directory, 91

H

Hanks, Tom, 22
head shots, 14–17, 19, 29
Henson, Jim, 125
Henson Productions, 128
How the Grinch Stole Christmas
      (film), 104

K

key grip, 88, 89

L

LeBlanc, Matt, 17
lighting technicians, 89, 92
location manager, 81, 83–85
location scouts, 80–87
    directory, 86–87
Los Angeles, 10, 19, 21, 53

M

makeup artist, 103–107
    directory, 106–107
    training, 105–106
Muppets, 125
Murphy, Eddie, 104

N

narrators, 37
New York City, 10, 19, 21
Nutty Professor II, The (film), 104

P

photography, 14–17
production assistants, 66–70
    directory, 69–70
    salaries, 67
production designers, 135
puppeteers, 125–131
    directory, 128–130
    training, 128
puppetry, 109

R

résumés, 17–19
Roberts, Julia, 22

S

SAG (Screen Actors Guild), 21, 31, 47, 53
Screen Actors Guild (SAG), 21, 31, 47, 53
Screen Extras Guild, 53
screenplays, 59–62
screenwriters, 58–65
    directory, 63–65
    training, 62
script supervisors, 71–79
    directory, 78–79
    training, 77–78
scriptwriters, 58–65
Seinfeld, Jerry, 22
Sesame Street (series), 126
sound effects, 119–123
special effects artists, 108–113, 125
    directory, 112–113
    training, 111–112
Star Trek (series), 97
Star Wars (film), 109, 126
stop motion animation, 114–115
studio writers, 62
stuntpersons, 44–51
    directory, 49–51
    training, 47–49
suit performers, 127–128

T

talent agents, 19–20, 28–35, 39
    directory, 33–35
    salaries, 31
    training, 33
Titanic (film), 72, 97

trade magazines, 15, 21, 25–26
Travolta, John, 22

U
unions, 21, 31, 47, 53

V
Variety (trade journal), 15, 26
voice overs, 37, 40, 41, 42
voice talent, 36–43
   agents, 39
   directory, 41–43
   training, 40–41

voice tapes, 37, 40

W
wardrobe, 96–102
   directory, 102
   salaries, 101
   training, 100–101
Watson, Sandy, 16, 19
Wizard of Oz, The (film), 74
Wonder Years, The (series), 37
writers, 58–65
   directory, 63–65
   training, 59, 62

About the Author

Melanie Ann Apel holds a bachelor's degree in theater arts from Bradley University. Her credits include both stage and industrial film acting as well as stage directing. Melanie lives in Chicago with her husband, Michael, and their brand new baby boy. She has written more than 30 books for the Rosen Publishing Group.

Acknowledgments

The author wishes to thank Darwin R. Apel, Esme Codell, Bonnie Juettner, members of the SCBWI, and especially Sandy Watson, for their expertise, guidance, and assistance. Without them this book could not have been completed.

Photo Credits

Cover © Adam Woolfitt/Corbis; pp. 11, 13 © John A. Rizzo/Photodisc; pp. 15, 52, 54 © Daniel Hulshizer/AP Wide World Photos; pp. 28, 30 © Ellen Denuto/Index Stock Imagery, Inc.; pp. 36, 38 © Kevin Wolf/AP Wide World Photos; pp. 44, 46 © Neal Preston/Corbis; p. 48 © *The News-Gazette*, Robert K. O'Daniell/AP Wide World Photos; pp. 58, 60 © Jules Frazier/PhotoDisc; pp. 66, 68 © Gjon Mili/TimePix; pp. 71, 73 © Ken Chernus/FPG; p. 76 © *The Tennessean*, Randy Piland/AP Wide World Photos; pp. 80, 82 © Wides + Holl/FPG; p. 84 © Garry Mitchell/AP Wide World Photos; pp. 88, 90 © Van Redin/TimePix; pp. 92, 94 © Jake Schoellkopf/AP Wide World Photos; pp. 96, 98 © Carlo Mavagnoli/TimePix; p. 100 © Kelly-Mooney Photography/Corbis; pp. 103, 104 © Jerome Delay/AP Wide World Photos; pp. 105, 110, 114, 116, 127 © The Everett Collection; pp. 108, 111 © Roger Ressmeyer/Corbis; pp. 119, 121 © Arthur S. Aubry/PhotoDisc; pp. 125, 126 © Reuters/TimePix; pp. 132, 135 © *The Daily Times*, Stephen Cherry/AP Wide World Photos; p. 134 © Shelley Gazin/Corbis.

Design and Layout

Evelyn Horovicz